Sex and Alcohol in Retirement

Alan Rose

Order this book online at www.trafford.com
or email orders@trafford.com

Most Trafford titles are also available at major online book retailers.

Printed in the United States of America.

ISBN: 978-1-4269-0051-8 (sc)
ISBN: 978-1-4669-0209-1 (e)

Because of the dynamic nature of the Internet, any web addresses or links contained in
this book may have changed since publication and may no longer be valid. The views
expressed in this work are solely those of the author and do not necessarily reflect the
views of the publisher, and the publisher hereby disclaims any responsibility for them.

Any people depicted in stock imagery provided by Thinkstock are models,
and such images are being used for illustrative purposes only.
Certain stock imagery © Thinkstock.

Trafford rev. 01/02/2015

 www.trafford.com

North America & international
toll-free: 1 888 232 4444 (USA & Canada)
fax: 812 355 4082

Acknowledgements

I am grateful to many for having supported me in the writing of this book, but to none more than my dear wife, Jean, who was a constant support, and also painted the front cover.

It would not have been possible to have written part one of this book without the use of the scrapbook made by my Daughter-in-law Leigh at the time at which the events took place. It proved to be a mine of accurate information and I am grateful to her.

Dr. Kasidas who started out many years ago as my research technician and eventually graduated in biochemistry and went on to obtain a D. Phil degree, was my continuous assistant in my research laboratory, and became a good friend. His help with the alcohol loading tests was invaluable, and I think that this was a unique double act in the drink-driving field.

Dr. Peter Liu was anther of my former employees who Became a good friend. He contributed a lot in my research activities, and later we worked together very amicably in the gender choice   clinics. He and his family extended great hospitality during my stay in Hong Kong..

It was a pleasure to work with Dr. Anthony Wong when he took over the clinic from Peter Liu. He and his family also proved extremely hospitable., Anthony proved supportive when I had to appear before the GMC of Hong Kong.

Alan Rose, Summer 2009

Preface

When I retired from the the National Health Service at the at the age of 65 in 1990 I expected to have little professional work to do. Having been a Chemical Pathologist for 25 years and in charge of both a routine and research laboratory I would be unable to function in the private field without a large laboratory at my disposal and this was clearly impossible.. True I had a small medicolegal practice in the drink-driving field but I thought that this would gradually dwindle away as news of my retirement spread.

How different was the way things turned out. First I met an old friend and former colleague in a queue for the theatre. He explained that he was working in Oman and they needed a person such as myself to work there. He persuaded the authorities there to invite me to be visiting Professor in biochemistry for a 3 month contract to give lectures and general advice. With my wife and son we travelled to Oman by air on the night that the land battle began in the first Gulf War After a thoroughly enjoyable 3 months we returned to London.

Next I bumped into another friend who had been my employee who told me about his proposal to start a clinic for choosing the sex of an anticipated baby. As described later this started a storm of publicity the like of which I had never previously experienced. It was this that eventually gave me the idea of publishing my experiences in this activity. I thought that it would be of interest to anyone who might think of setting up a clinic in a sensitive area to see how to cope with the opposition and publicity that can arise, and how one has to overcome these problems.

To my surprise the medicolegal work grew considerably over the next few years and kept me quite busy producing reports for solicitors and travelling to many parts of England and Wales to give expert evidence to the courts of law. However, my health is now is now a source of worry and as a result the legal

work is dwindling at long last and it occurred to me that it would

also be of interest to motorists and perhaps others to read about

my work in this area. Therefore I have combined my two main

retirement activities into one volume. The title "sex and alcohol

in retirement" seems appropriate and accurate, but will not

I hope be misleading.

Contents

Section one. The London Gender Clinic

Part two; alcohol

A. How did it all happen?

The publicity when it came was like a tsunami. Our new clinic had been open a week and suddenly we were front page news headlines and lead items on the TV news not only in the UK but also overseas. I was being whisked from news room to newsroom. There were questions in Parliament and even an early day motion in the House of Commons, trying to close the just-opened clinic. The telephone scarcely stopped at the clinic for a month.

Having worked for 25 years as a NHS consultant, I retired on my 65 th birthday as required. Soon afterwards I was invited to the Sultan Qaboos University Hospital in Oman as a visiting Professor for three months. The stay was thoroughly enjoyable but when I was offered a three-year contract, I graciously declined, and returned to the UK to contemplate quiet retirement.

The clinic was really the brainchild of Dr. Peter Liu., a man of considerable initiative. He was born in Hong Kong but came to the UK and obtained a degree in Chemistry at Imperial College London, followed by a Doctorate in Philosophy. I first met   Peter some 10 years earlier when I had advertised For a Chemist take charge of analysis of alcohol in body fluids in a private laboratory in which I then had an interest.. There were about a hundred replies, but I was impressed by Peter's initiative in   simply walking in and applying on the spot   After doing the job in a highly satisfactory manner for a year or so he resigned to look into other commercial activities.

A year or two later still I managed to entice him to be a part of my research team in my NHS laboratory (Actually part of the Institute of Urology) to undertake an abstruse piece of Biochemical research. Again, he delivered as I had hoped and two or three research papers followed. Peter resigned at about the same time as my retirement from the NHS in 1990.

1. Proposal for a new clinic

We met again after I retired by a chance encounter in the street. After exchanging pleasantries he said that he wanted to set up a clinic for determining what the sex of a baby would be, and he thought he ought to have a Medical Doctor to help him, and as I was not working would I be interested. I agreed to look into what had been published on the subject and Peter gave me all the papers to read. It transpired that there were already some 50 or so such clinics which had been operating in the USA for up to 15 years, and a recent large study had reported 80% success rate in forming males when that sex had been requested.   What impressed me even more was that in a country as litiginous as the USA, there seemed to have been no claims for wrong sex or other reasons. There were no such clinics in the UK or in the rest of Europe and Peter thought that the time was right to open a clinic in London The method was a biochemical treatment of the sperm of the husband followed by artificial insemination of the Wife. It seemed to me that Peter

was especially qualified to carry out the biochemical part and I

agreed to see the couples beforehand to establish their

suitability for the procedures and generally supervise the

medical aspects. The chemicals required were available from a

commercial firm in the USA headed by Dr. Ericcson who had

pioneered the method.

2. He threatened to have me struck off the medical register.

Soon after starting at Central Pathology Laboratories, I received a telephone call from an eminent Professor of Pathology at a famous London Teaching Hospital. He invited me to dine with him at the prestigious Athanaeum Club in Pall Mall. When I accepted he went on to explain that he wanted to tell me why he proposed to ask the General Medical Council to have me struck off the medical register. The luncheon was not very good and far from enjoyable while he outlined his Complaints. I can only remember one of them, namely that The name of the laboratory appeared in the London telephone directory, albeit in the normal small type in alphabetical order. This seemed to me to be quite absurd, as indeed were the rest of his complaints

Having finished lunch, my next stop, was the nearest telephone kiosk where I made a call to the Medical Defence

Union (MDU) to explain the details of the Professor's complaints. I was quickly assured that they would not stand, and that if he went ahead, which they doubted, the MDU would give me full support. In fact I heard no more of this matter, and I was left wondering what the Professor's motives had been. It was not the first of April, and if it was a joke, it was rather an expensive one for him.

3. Were there any legal problems?

Peter had already been busy on this matter and discovered

That a licence was required only if;--

1. Sperm or seminal fluid were to be frozen and stored
    .
    on the premises or elsewhere. Since sperm samples were

    to be treated and inseminated all in one day, this did not

    apply..

11. If artificial insemination by donor was contemplated, a

    licence would be required. However we proposed only

    to inseminate between husband & wife, or partner if in a

    long and stable relationship) It had been realized for

    many years that artificial insemination   between husband

    and wife could not be banned for obvious reasons and

    therefore a licence to permit the insemination was not

    required

4 . Preliminary consultations with authorities.

Being legal is one thing, but would the powers that be have objections. I therefore consulted a number of the relevant authorities;–

   i. General Medical Council. They   wrote and told me that they were   there to interpret the public will and as they did not know what the public will was on this matter would be, they could give no advice. I found it quite remarkable that this   august body would duck the question, rather than take a lead and give some guidance. However I took this to mean that they had no objection to the clinic opening.

ii. The British Medical Association. They first objected on the grounds that the treatment was not 100% successful. I replied that I did not know of any treatments   that were 100 % successful.

Second, they though it would increase the abortion

rate. I pointed out that on the contrary, It would reduce the abortion rate since this was sometimes performed because of the foetus having the sex that was not wanted. Later, when the furore broke after the clinic opened, the BMA called a public meeting with various speakers taking part. I was not allowed to be a main speaker but was allowed to be present and ask questions. After I explained the guide lines on which we proposed to be bound by (more of this later) the meeting ended with a unanimous vote that the clinic should be permitted to operate. However that did not end the matter as far as the BMA was concerned. They referred the issue to their ethics committee who again approved that the opening of the clinic should be allowed. At the following AGM of the BMA, they rejected the recommendations of their own ethics committee. In reply I said that the BMA was quite undemocratic because the Doctors who attended the AGM were those with the time to do so and these are mostly the elderly age group and were "Fuddy-duddies" and not representatives of the BMA doctors as a whole. In any case the resolutions of the BMA carried no legal weight.

iii The Medical Defence Union

Without their agreement to accept my insurance there was no possibility that I would take part in the venture. At first they were reluctant, but I pointed out what my role would be, and also that I would not share in the profits of the clinic, but simply take a standard fee for interviewing the couples and either allow them to go ahead or refuse them, and my word would be final. After a considerable delay, during which the matter was considered by their highest committee they approved my insurance.

iv. The Human fertilisation and embryologyauthority

We did not officially consult this body because we were not going to freeze sperm or keep it on the premises, and since we were only treating married couples, we would be outside their terms of reference.

V. The Royal College of Obstetrics and Gynaecology.

I never had a reply, and so took that to mean that they had no objection to the proposed clinic.

B. Our Self imposed ethical guide lines.

There now seemed no reasons for not opening the clinic and we took the decision to go ahead.   Peter Liu was very concerned that the clinic should be seen to be run on ethical lines, and to that end right from day 1 we agreed the following guide lines;--

A. We would only accept for treatment   families with at least one child already.

B. We would only accept attempts to balance the sex of sex of the babies in any given family.

C. We would only accept for treatment married couples or couples who could show a stable relationship of some years.

D. In order to substantiate the information we would want to see marriage certificate, and birth certificates of all the offsprings

E.   Both   husband   and   wife   would   always   be
interviewed by me together, so that each partner
knew that they had been given identical
information,

f. Artificial insemination would always be performed
By a female trained nurse.

g. Only one sample of sperm should be on the premises
at one time. This would make a mix up of samples
impossible. I had   been   working in hospital
laboratories for long enough to know that people
sometimes have aberrations resulting in   samples
being swapped. In fact, this was one of the greatest
fears of couples who dreaded the thought that
the wife might be inseminated with the wrong
sperm. I was able to swear that such a mix-up
was not only unlikely, but impossible.

h. We also used disposable tubes and pipettes, to be used once and thrown away before the next sample of sperm was handled. Therefore we could not have any cross-contamination of samples, as was tragically reported in IVF treatment in Holland.

Finally, but of great importance, each couple treated had to sign an undertaking not to abort the foetus if it was found to have the sex they did not want. Some said that this was worthless, but in fact we asked each treated couple to inform us when a pregnancy was achieved and to tell us the sex as soon as it was known, and the final outcome at birth. In this way it became clear that there were extremely few abortions.

C. How did the public react?

There was a mostly negative response from the public at first, which was not altogether surprising considering the way in which the press reported the event. The medical profession did not comment very much with the exception of the BMA (see above). A well known IVF expert said that although Dr. Rose was "plausible" there was no evidence that the method really worked, and in any case he opposed the procedure on moral grounds. However, since this was the very man who had first opposed IVF when it came into use, but then embraced the method and became a leading authority on its use, I felt that his opinion might change with time., and therefore should not carry much weight

On the other hand there were a few influential magazines that supported the clinic, notably the Economist., and in the issue of January 30th to February 5th 1993 made the point that if a group feels that a certain procedure is immoral, but does no harm, while the group was free to ban the technique being used by its members, it should not proscribe it for others with different beliefs.

There were a number of radio and TV programmes on which some strange ideas were put forward. Usually they dealt with the subject in superficial ways, but there was one notable exception. Brian Hayes chaired a 2-hour radio debate with questions phoned in by the public in which he would not accept for discussion frivolous questions.

A number of good points were discussed. Some thought that the clinic was "playing God" by interfering with nature. My response was that was exactly what Doctors did when they saved lives by giving drugs such as antibiotics, or, by removing an inflamed appendix, or carrying out a Caesarean Section to save the life of a baby.

Another objection was "a gut feeling" that there was some-thing wrong about influencing the sex of a baby. I replied that I could not deal with gut feelings; if people could not articulate the basis for their feelings I could not respond.

Another cause of disquiet was the thought that the balance of the sexes in the general population could be altered by extensive use of sex selection. My response was that there were much more enjoyable ways of creating babies other than the use of IVF or our procedure, and only a small proportion of the population would opt for sex selection. This proportion Would be further reduced by our policy of;—

1. Not treating for a first baby.

2. Only treating to balance the sexes in any given family

Any alterations in the small subset of the population that we were treating would hardly effect the whole population..

Other objectors.

There was a small group of MP's who took strong objections to the clinic. The MP for Hendon North, Mr. Marshall was strongly opposed. He was quoted in the Edgware & Mill Hill Times as having said "I'm appalled that parents seek to play God with nature. The London Gender Clinic can not even guarantee success". I wrote a letter to him, inviting him to come and see how the clinic operated, and to hear about our guide lines, but he declined to accept the offer.

David Amiss was an MP for Basildon with strong objections .and proposed an early day motion in the House of Commons , that was designed to stop the clinic in its tracks.

Early day motion in the House of Commons on 23rd February 1993 introduced by David Amiss, MP for Basildon "to prohibit the use of techniques designed to influence the sex of a foetus at conception"..

voting for the motion were;–

Richard Alexander, Michael Allison, David Alton, David Amess, Michael Ancram, Donald Anderson, Jacques Arnold, David Atkinson, Robert Banks, Rt Hon. A.J.Beith Vivian Bendall, Joe Benton, Andrew Bowden, Sir Rhodes Boyson, Julian Brazier, Angela Browning, Menzies Campbell, D.N.Campbell-Savours, Paul Channon, Mr. Churchill, James Clappison, Michael Colvin, David Congdon, Anthony Coombs, Cynog Dafis, Quentin Davies, Stephen Day, Nirj Joseph Deva, Alan Duncan, Harold Elletson, Jonathan Evans, David Evennett, David Faber, Dame Peggy Fenner, Dr. Liam Fox, Sir Marcus Fox, Peter Fry, Phil Gallis, Christopher Gill. Harry Greenway, Sir Michael Gylls, David Harris, Warren Hawksley, Simon Hughes, Toby Jessel, Dame Elaine Kellett-Bowman, Sir James Killedder, Angela Knight, Dame Jill Knight, Sir Ivan Lawrence, David Livington, Michael Lord, Liz Lynne, Thomas McAvoy, Calum Macdonald, Lady Olga Maitland, David Marshall, Sir Michael Marshall, Michael J. Martin, James Molyneux, Sir Fergus Montgomery, Sir Michael Neubert, David Nicholson, James Pawsey, Elizabeth Peacock, David Porter, William Powell, Andrew Robathan, Marion Roe, William Ross, Colin Shepherd, Sir Trevor Skeet, Sir Dudley Smith, Rev Martin Smyth, Sir Keith Speed, Sir James Spicer, David Sumberg, Matthew Taylor, Roy Thomason, Richard, Tracey, David Trimble, Paul Tyler, Gary Waller, Nigel Waterson, John Wittingdale, Ann Winterton.

Opposition to the motion was led by Glenda Jackson, and **Voting against i**t were;–

-Diane Abbott, Graham Allen, Hilary Armstrong, John Austin-Walker, Tony Banks, Harry Barnes, Kevin Barron, Andrew F Bennett, David Blunkett, Peter Bottomley, Keith Bradley, N. Brown, Richard Burden, Stephen Byers, Anne Campbell, Malcolm Chisholm, David Clark, Ann Glywd, Harry Cohen, Michael Connerty, Frank Cook, Jeremy Corbin, Jean Corston, Tom Cox, Bob Cryer, John Cummings, Lawrence Cunliffy, Rt. Hon John Cunningham, Tam Dalyell, Alistair Darling, Ian Davidson, Bryan Davies, Rt Hon Denzil Davies, John Denham, Frank Dobson, Bill Etherington, John Evans, Margaret Ewing, Derek Falchett, Mark Fisher, Paul Flynn, Rt Hon Derek Foster, John Fraser, John Garrett, Bruce George, Neil Gerrard, Neil Gerrard, Llin Golding, Teresa Gorman, Win Griffiths,unnell, Peter Hain, Mike Hall, Peter Hardy, Harriet Harman, Doug Henderson, Keith Hill, Kate Hoey, John Home Robertson, Jimmy Hoodo, Geoffrey Hoon, Doug Hoyle Kevin Hughes, John Hutton, Glenda Jackson, Helen Jackson, Lynne Jones, Tessa Jowell, Alan Keen, Jane Kennedy, Piara S Khabra, Peter Kilfoyle, Archy Kirkwood, Jacqui Lait, Joan Lestor, Terry Lewis, Ken Livingstone, Elfin Llwyd, Eddie Loyden, William McKelvey, Max Madden, Bill Michie, Alan Milburn, Elliot Morley, Estelle Morris, Marjorie Mowlam, Chris Mullen, Martin O'Neil, Colin Picthall, Bridget Prentice, Dawn Primarolo, Joyce Quinn, Barbara Roche, Terry Rooney, Ernie Rose, Joan Ruddock, Brian Sedgemore, Dennis Skinner, C. Smith, Clive Soley, Rt Hon David Steel, Jack Straw, Paddy Tipping. Joan Walley, David Winnick, Audrey Wise.

Clearly the motion was defeated with 106 votes against 87 ayes. That put an end to organised objections. .However it did not silence David Amiss whom I was to meet later when we both spoke at a Cambridge Union debate. In an aside to me he said that one day he would have the clinic closed. He was somewhat taken aback when I informed him that his constituents were coming to the clinic in significant numbers. Needless to say, his threat was an empty gesture and he never did succeed in halting the progress of the clinic. May be this was in his thoughts when he gave up his Parliamentary seat at Basildon and moved to another area.

E. The press

Just before the clinic opened we inquired from the local newspaper, the Hendon & Finchley Times as to what they might charge for a small advertisement. They responded by sending a reporter to find out what we were proposing to do, and I explained what we were about. That was on about 19th January, 1993. Two days later our local Times carried the banner headline on its front page;--

Battle of the sexes

Clinic lets parents choose the sex of their baby

On January 22nd 1993 the Daily Mail carried a banner headline on its front page;--

"Pick sex of your Baby Row"

On January 22nd 1993 the Daily Express headline was

Now you can choose the sex of your baby

Uproar as scientist launch new clinic

And the Evening Standard chose;--

Choosing your baby's sex won't harm mother nature

On Saturday 23rd January 1993 the main headline on the Front page of the Times was;–

Sex selection birth clinic prompts wave of protest.

While the daily Telegraph sported;--

Legal loophole frees sex selection clinic.

And the Independent said;--

British attitude "is arrogant hogwash"

Clinics in the US have been using sex selection for almost 20 years.

And the debate carried on for over a week. I was swamped with invitations to appear on TV and this too proved an interesting experience. Alistair Stuart, the well know ITV news reader interviewed me live at the start of the 6 PM news. His opening question was, Dr. Rose are you not in this for the money? Me, well are you not too in your job for the money? After the news he took me aside and explained that he was just doing his job and I should not be offended by his opening question. He was so charming that I said that I was not offended.

There were good things and bad things about the behaviour of the press. First, we were given publicity that we could never have achieved in any other way. As a result the telephone line was continually ringing with couples asking for appointments.. The phone was in constant use, day and night, and we soon had a six month waiting list. Our family members rallied round. to help take down names and addresses and phone numbers, and sending out information.

But with free publicity from the press, there also came a curse. In these early days, there was frantic activity at the clinic. There were reporters and inspectors milling around, and one day my daughter (a trained nurse at that time) was taking all the

.

phone calls and writing the information on a pad.. In the light of what followed it became apparent that one reporter had memorised two names and telephone numbers of prospective clients. Now we were always quite specific that all information about clients would be completely confidential. Imagine my horror when we were telephoned by two couples each giving the same story. They alleged that a woman with a broad Scottish accent had telephoned purporting to be from the London Gender Clinic and asking for personal and intimate details. Subsequently this information was printed in their local newspapers. Needless to say the couples were more than somewhat distressed. I assured them it was none of our doing, but I knew there was a reporter with a broad Scottish accent who must have been responsible. I wrote to the press complaints commission, only to have them reply that they could not act unless they were contacted directly by the complainees. They however had had enough of publicity and wanted no more and declined to take the matter further.

.   There were other problems with the press. Come what may they simply refused to mention our strict guidelines, so that the public were not properly informed about our ethical code of practice.. Also their ideas on photography were annoying. They never took one photo, but took a whole series of shots of Peter and myself, and the editor chose which one would be published. It seemed to me that they always chose the least flattering one.

Having observed the behaviour of the press, I fully expected one or more reporters to pose as couples seeking the help of the clinic. In fact I thought to have this happen on two occasions. In both cases the couples were European, and about 30 years of age; The woman did most of the talking and the man showed very little interest in what I had to say. I treated them in the usual way, carefully explaining the procedure, the risks and benefits of what we could do. It was satisfying that I never saw or heard of in the press an article describing what A reporter might have learned about our activities.

F. The results

A. Social.

Couples came from all over the UK, and from many European countries, Scandinavia, from the middle East, India, Pakistan, and Australia. It was not my business to enquire into their religious beliefs, but they often surfaced during the interviews. It was clear that they included Church of England, Catholics, Hindus and Moslems. I never knowingly saw a Jewish couple, although I can not exclude the possibility that there were a few. Couples came from all economic classes from quite poor people to peers of the realm, and indeed overseas royalty.

The social aspects of the first 809 couples were reviewed in the referreed journal "Human Reproduction", volume 10, pages 968 to 971.

Of the 809 couples ;--

> 57.8% were of Indian origin,
> 32% European,
> 3.6% Chinese and
> 6.8% of other ethnic origins.

Within the total 809 couples interviewed 37.5% were treated.. The high drop out rate seemed to me to indicate that the couples understood the limitations of the procedure and had therefore opted out. This was a cause of satisfaction.

In the group of 809 couples interviewed, those wanting boys were;--

Indian couples 96%
European couples 38.4%
Chinese couples 89.75
Other couples 90.9 %

showing a contrast between European couples and the others as has been found in other studies in the USA.

Three other interesting facts emerged from this data. First,

the mean age of the wives was about 35 years in all groups and often this was to be the last try for a baby. We had no pregnancies in wives over the age of 41 years, even though a few wanted to try for a baby by our procedure even after I warned them that that the chances of a pregnancy were extremely unlikely.

Second, in the Indian group wanting boys for example the average number of girls already in the family was 2.75 . This shows that there is only a small subset of the Indian population that asked for boys and this should be reassuring to those that fear a large distortion in the sex ratio of boys to girls in the whole population. One couple came from the Yemen and had had 10 girls and no boys. Although we treated for a boy this was one of the few couples from whom we never heard again.

Third, 80.6% said at interview that even if the clinic had not existed they would have tried to have another baby without the possibility of sex choice.

G. The Hong Kong Gender Choice Centre.

Introduction.

Peter Liu came to the UK at the age of 3, but still had family in Hong Kong and in about the middle of the summer of 1993 told me of his ambition to set up a gender choice centre in Hong Kong. Would I be prepared to go with him to Hong Kong to open another such clinic to be run on similar lines to those in Hendon? I said that I would be agreeable to go for a period of up to 4 months. We agreed that for a time we would close the clinic in Hendon to new couples from the time of Peter's departure until his return and couples would be given the option of going on to a waiting list.

Peter went out first in order to find a suitable building and to furnish it and to find living quarters for me. I followed in October 1993. He chose a building in Wellington Street on Hong Kong Island which is in a good commercial area. As mentioned above, the London Gender Clinic had been in a house in a suburb of London and which he owned However, the press were not very flattering about the general decor of those premises and he was determined not to have the same criticism in Hong Kong where "face" was important. He took an area on the 14th Floor of the building and decorated and furnished it tastefully and fit for purpose.

When I arrived in Hong Kong it was nearing completion but there was nowhere suitable for me to stay on Hong Kong Island, where accommodation was extremely expensive. Peter would not let a problem like this deter him. His solution was to install   a convertible divan bed in the consulting room of the clinic, and to provide enough wardrobe space, and for me to have the use of the bathroom and toilet when not in use during the working day. This would have the advantage of providing me with comfortable living space rent free and without any commut-ing problem. For the first few days I lived in hotels off the Island,and then in a flat of a relative of Peter. After a week or two

I was able to move into the new premises where I found that the arrangements worked worked admirably. My working day went like this;--

8 AM Get dressed, wash etc.

8.30 AM go out for breakfast; Good choice of eateries.

9.00 AM make up bed into divan mode and tidy room.

9.30 AM ready to receive staff and patients

6.00 PM. Working day finished.
Enter details of day's new patients on to the computer.

7.00 PM Prepare to go out for evening meal, or other leisure activities. Radio, TV available in clinic.

11.00 PM Convert divan and retire.

Before the clinic opened I was able to see how work proceeded on the offices. I noticed that every detail of the planning was thoroughly thrashed out in lengthy discussions. Work proceeded at high speed. At one point the marble top for the reception desk was being put in place when I noticed a sharp edge at a corner. On mentioning this, immediately, and with no further discussion, it was removed, rounded off and put back, all in under an hour.

H. Opening of the Gender Choice Centre,

The centre opened in mid November 1993. It was staffed

by;–

Peter liu & myself, plus

laboratory manager Polly Chum, a relative of Peter who
had studied biochemistry, and helped with the
sperm separations

Business manager Kam, another relative of Peter.

Bessie, a registered nurse who would perform the inseminations.. Bessie had been trained in insemination techniques and had a good CV. She acted as my interpreter when I interviewed couples with limited English. On one occasion when I was smitten with the common cold she brought me in some snake soup which she assured me would cure the cold, I tasted it with some trepidation but found it was rather like chicken soup, and so took my medicine. Lo and behold the cold got better! Another time she wanted to write my horoscope but although I knew the year and the month and the date of my birth, I did not know the time, and so this threat was avoided.

Staff of Gender Choice Centre in Hong Kong
Left tor right—

       Kam, Business manager.
       Author
       Polly Chum, Biochemist
       Winnie Liu
       Peter liu, Owner
       Dr. Ericsson

The opening of the Gender Choice Centre was accompanied by a publicity storm rather similar to what we had experienced in London. The Hong Kong Medical Association called an open public meeting to consider the matter. Peter was invited to attend and speak. However, I think that Peter made an important strategic error by declining to attend. As explained above, Peter came to the UK at the age of 3 years and as a result his Cantonese was not as fluent as he would have liked. It was modesty concerning his ability to speak elegantly in Cantonese. I felt that this would be no impediment but he felt differently and consequently the opportunity to address the critics of the clinic was lost. Nevertheless, there was a steady flow of clients. Most of them had little or no English and I had to have an interpreter in order to interview them. Sometimes Bessie took over in the role of interpreter. The worries they had were very similar to those I had interviewed in London. The striking thing was that most of the couples were Chinese and they overwhelmingly wanted a boy, having had several girls already.

A

Front page of the South China
Sunday Morning Post on
7th November 1993

Some couples came from mainland China and invariably were able to prove that they already had one or more girls. I enquired about the "one child" policy but they then explained that this only applied to the poor and not to the rich. The reason for this was that if there was more than one child in the family they would cease to be eligible for state benefits such as free education and health services. While this was a stern threat to the poor, it held no terrors for the rich who could afford private education and private medicine. I was asked once what I thought about the communist regime in China. I replied that I thought it was a joke to talk about a communist regime which harboured on the one hand millions of impoverished people, and on the other hand, a large number of millionaires. This reply was met with stoney-faced silence.

I. Brought before the General Medical Council of Hong Kong.

To my surprise and consternation I received a letter from the GMC of Hong Kong indicating that I was to appear before the disciplinary committee to answer the charge of having advertised inappropriately.. The basis of the charge was that in inserting an advertisement in the local press , as was permitted to a doctor setting up a new practice, I had violated the rule which states that while the address and date of opening may be given, the speciality should definitely not be given.

My crime was that in stating the name of the centre as "Gender Choice Centre" as part of the address (see fig 2), I had stated the speciality. My defence was that the public needed to know the name of the centre to able to find it in the large tower block which housed it.

I immediately wrote to the Medical Defence Union in London who agreed to appoint an eminent solicitor in Hong Kong to undertake this task. When the day of the hearing came

GCC

GENDER CHOICE CENTRE

(Wholly owned subsidiary of Gender Choice Ltd.)

Dr. G. A. Rose MA (OXON) BM BCh (OXON) DM (OXON) FRCP (U.K.) FRCPath (U.K.) FRSC (U.K.)

Medical Advisor

Room 901, 8/F Sin Hua Bank Building,
19 Wellington Street,
Central, Hong Kong.
Tel: (852) 868 6820   Fax: (852) 523 7277

Consultation Hours:
Mon-Fri 10:00am to 6:00pm
Sat 10:00am to 2:00pm
Sun & Public Holidays Closed
(Treatment may be possible
by special arrangement)

Business card card showing not only the address, but also the speciality of the clinic. The alleged offence was to combine these two items into the advertisement placed in the local newspapers. Nowadays that is permitted but it was deemed an offence in 1993

many months later I was a little nervous because my barrister had agreed that in fact technically I was guilty although there were mitigating circumstances.

The hearing took about 2 hours of the afternoon, during which I was treated with some respect as a senior member of the medical profession. It was accepted that I had not intended to breach the ethical code, but as I had in fact done so I was technically guilty. They imposed the minimum punishment that they could, namely an un-gazetted reprimand. The press were waiting for me when I emerged to ask me what I thought about the matter, but acting on advice I kept my mouth firmly shut.

I was interested to hear some time later that the rule I had infringed was deleted and in future the speciality of the doctor could be included, a reform that I deemed sensible.

J. Comparing results for boys in London & Hong Kong

While Peter was in Hong Kong we could not continue to run the clinic in London, and the latter was therefore temporarily closed and couples who enquired were told that they would have to wait until we reopened, probably three or four months later.

It was intended that the biochemical processing of the sperm should be the same in both laboratories, both being set up by Peter. However, Peter was planning that when he re turned to London, the sperm separation would be left in the hands of another capable biochemist, namely Polly, while my job of interviewing couples would be transferred to a local Doctor. Later, Peter sold his share in the Hong Kong clinic to a local biochemist, Anthony Wong. T hus the two clinics could operate simultaneously.

Every three or 4 months I returned to Hong Kong to see how things were going. After a time it came apparent to me that results for boys in Hong Kong were considerably better than in London. On close inspection of the meticulously kept records of details of the sperm separation techniques another fact emerged. While Hong Kong was sticking to the recommendation that the percentage of sperm transferred to the uterus should not exceed 5% of the original total, in London the percentage used had been increased to try and increase the conception rate. A recent research paper from the USA had confirmed the necessity to stick to the 5% rule. Peter then adopted the 5% rule and following this The London success rate , matched the Hong Kong success rate of 83% so exceeding our advertised 80% for the method.

L. Success rate for girls.

It soon became apparent that the success rate for girls was not satisfactory in London, while in Hong Kong it was impossible to assess the success rate since there were virtually no couples opting for this sex. We t herefore stopped offering the treatment for girls until a new technique was developed in the USA by the Microsort organisation situated in Fairfax, Virginia, just outside Washington DC. The new technique was completely different from the method we had bee using. It involved;–

1. Staining the chromosomes in the seminal fluid with a fluorescent dye.

2. Passing a stream of individual sperm one at a time though a gate during which it would be exposed to ultraviolet light which would make the chromosomes fluoresce. The colour which the stain then shows depends on the X or Y chromosome.

3 The colour of the sperm determined in which direction

the sperm would move after passing through the gate.

In contrast with the Ericsson albumin method which we used, there were several steps which were potentially harmful to the sperm;–

1. Exposure of the chromosomes to a dye.

2. Exposure to ultraviolet light.

Although the dye was thought to be harmless and exposure to ultraviolet was for only a tiny fraction of a second, and the method had been applied to at least three generations of several animal species with no ill effects having been noted, the USA had allowed only one centre to be licensed to use this technique on human beings. However, when they did so the results showed over 90%, success rate for girls.

Peter and I went over to the USA to visit the laboratory in Fairfax, Virginia. I gave a lecture there and it soon became apparent that they had excellent facilities and they had adopted guide-lines for selection and treatment of couples almost identical to ours, but with one important difference. Whereas we had kept to our original decision to have only sample on the premises at ay one time, they took the view that this was not economic, and instead used a very carefully designed system of identifying the samples. Nevertheless, we came to an arrangement whereby we would select couples in London who wanted to have girls and carry out all the preliminary tests in our clinic in Hendon and then send the couples for treatment in Fairfax. I carefully explained to each couple the potential risks involved and also why these were thought not to be a problem. It was then up to each couple to decide whether the new method was safe enough or not. Some chose safety and did not go ahead, while others were attracted to the new highly efficient method and chose to go to the USA.

M. Serendipity and a sting in the tail.

Serendipity means doing the right thing for the wrong reason, a phenomenon that has frequently occurred in medicine.. Peter had been anxious to investigate the procedure used for separation of sperm by the albumin columns used and to this end he had bought a fluorescent microscope. He first stained the sperm with dyes which made the X-sperm fluoresce green and the y-sperm fluoresce red when exposed to ultraviolet light. He examined sperm taken from subjects without the separation technique and from the sperm after passage through the albumin columns which should have shown enrichment with the X Sperm.

To avoid being influenced by knowing the sex of the foetus or baby, the Hong Kong clinic prepared slides of the sperm of individual men before and after passage through the albumin columns, also noting the sex of the baby born. The information accompanying the slides were identified by a code name only, so that Peter had no knowledge of which sperm he was examining and he was conducting a truly blind trial. Only when the trial was complete was the code broken and the results became clear, was the truth revealed. The results surprised us greatly. While samples from untreated men showed equal numbers of red and green sperm (I.e. "male" and"female") as was expected, The same result was found in those men who had been treated and subsequently had male babies. This clearly drove a coach and horses through the theory that passage through albumin resulted in separation of the male from the female sperm, and meant that although we were doing the right thing to obtain an apparent sperm separation, we were doing it for the wrong reason. This is a clear example of serendipity, but not the first time this has occurred in medical practice

We published this surprising result in the refereed

We would have liked to have extended this research work but the clinic was coming to the end and therefore we had to leave the matter for others to follow up.

N. Waning and closing of the London clinic

The publicity we received from the press was something we could not have afforded even if we had been allowed to advertise. However the press slowly lost interest in gender choice and moved on to other medical advances, such as cloning of animals, and this in resulted in a gradual dropping off in the numbers of patients enquiring and attending the clinic, and it was becoming uneconomic to continue. Also, Peter & I were becoming interested in other activities, so we took the decision to close the London clinic.

Peter eventually decided to move to Hong Kong and invest in the property market. I was finding that my medico - legal practice in the field of drink-driving cases was growing and taking up more of my time. This is described in part two of this book.

O. Developments in Hong Kong

Peter had sold his interest in the Hong Kong clinic to Anthony Wong, another competent and go-ahead biochemist. He too, eventually found that public interest was waning and decided to move on to other things. He, in collaboration with a local Doctor opened the first private IVF clinic in Hong Kong and also opened another IVF clinic in Mainland China.

Part two

Alcohol

P. How it came about.

At the end of a trial in which I had given expert evidence the prosecutor came over and said "I suppose Dr. Rose this is your hobby now" . In fact his shrewd observation was rather accurate and I agreed with him. I found that as retirement from the NHS progressed my acting as expert witness on drink and driving matters grew increasingly agreeable.

In 1969 I changed my NHS appointment from full time to maximum part-time consultant. This meant that I was free to take on private work and I took up a partnership in the Antigen Laboratories, which we renamed as Central Pathology Laboratories. As it happened this was just after the first drink-driving law had come into force and the lab had recently moved into the field of analysis of alcohol in blood and urine as a service to the general public. After retiring from the NHS this occupation expanded considerably and become "my hobby".

Q. Brief history of measurement of alcohol in blood urine and breath.

The development of the drink-driving laws became

possible because of corresponding scientific developments in

the ability to analyse alcohol in body fluids. Likewise the errors

in analysis also changed, and the grounds for legal defences also

changed. Therefore I have reviewed below how things

developed with time.

Although it had long been known that alcohol absorbed

into the body would find its way into breath it was not until 1938

that the first instrument, named the drunkometer, was invented

in which the alcohol content of breath was actually measured.

Breath was blown into a bag to provide a measured quantity

and this was subsequently blown into a solution of purple

potassium permanganate which was discoloured by the alcohol.

However, the second world war delayed developments in

the UK but eventually the road traffic act of 1967 empowered

the police to use what became known as the "Breathalyser ".

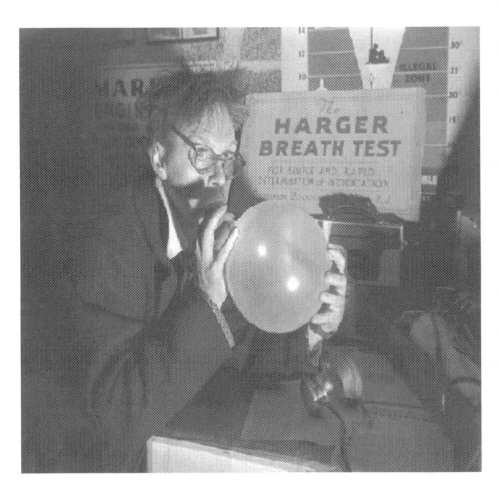

Original "Drunkometer"
Invented by Dr. Rolla N. Harger in 1931,
an Indiana University biochemist, and
adopted by Indiana Police in 1938 for
measuring breath alcohol (see text)

How the the Breathalyser worked ;-

1. The motorist blew into one end of a plastic bag to inflate it completely.

2. The Policeman then squeezed the breath through a tube at the other end of the bag, which contained crystals of orange potassium dichromate.

3. The alcohol in the breath reduced the orange colour to a green colour,

4. The colour change began at the beginning of the tube of crystals, and the extent of progress was determined by the amount of alcohol blown.

5. If the   line indicating the end of the orange zone and beginning of the green zone was beyond a certain distance the motorist was deemed to be over the legal limit for driving.

If the breath alcohol level was apparently over the legal limit the police were further empowered to request a sample

.of blood or urine to be analysed for alcohol by one of the methods in use at the time. If the motorist refused to give a sample he was liable to lose his driving licence.

When blood was taken it was divided between two small tubes, each containing anticoagulant, and filled with blood, one being kept for analysis by the police, and the other offered to the motorist who could then select an independent analyst My new private laboratory was on the list of recommended analysts and consequently received a regular supply of requests for private analysis.

Various problems arose with these procedures.

1. The dividing line between green and orange colours was not always as obvious as required to make a correct diagnosis and this was made worse by night-time conditions. Furthermore, it seemed that tobacco smoking could affect the result.

2. The blood samples taken sometimes clotted rendering accurate readings impossible. Blood outside the body quickly clots, and then the s a m p l e may be split into the red clot containing the red blood cells and a clear serum. The problem is that alcohol is dissolved only in the aqueous part of the blood, and as the red cells contain less water than does the same volume of serum, the concentration in 100 ml of serum is not the same as in 100 ml of whole blood, or as in 100 ml of red cells. Even worse, the difference between alcohol in 100 ml of serum and in 100 ml of blood depends upon the haemoglobin concentration and while this is fairly constant in the healthy it is different men and women. Therefore in order to apply a correct conversion factor the haemoglobin concentration needs to be known

As a result of these deficiencies in the methods many of the early court cases arose from either questioning the interpretation of the dividing line between the colours of the crystals, or on the fact that the blood sample was clotted so rendering impossible a true calculation of whole blood sample alcohol level.

However, the problem of the clotted sample was not solved immediately and in addition other problems arose. Thus, the ability of the breathalyser to distinguish between alcohol and Acetone was a problem with the early breathalysers. This gave rise to the "acetone defence" because acetone appears in the breath under two circumstances;–

1 It had long been known that in a prolonged fast, acetone can be detected by smelling the breath and in fact raises the apparent alcohol level measured.

2. The same thing occurred in untreated or under treated diabetics.

The "acetone defence " had frequently been used, some times successfully and sometimes not. The matter was often difficult for magistrates to understand and then they convicted, knowing full well that the matter could go to an appeal court, which might quash the conviction.

Then there was the problems of samples which had been apparently subjected to tampering;–

1. Normal blood had been injected into the tube so as to dilute the original sample and hence lower the apparent alcohol level.

2. The blood had been placed on a radiator to try and lower the alcohol content.

These are considered more fully below, page 72.

Analysis by gas chromatography.

Our private laboratory was already analysing for alcohol in blood by gas chromatography when I arrived on the scene. In this method the blood sample is diluted with water containing a fixed concentration of propanol as an internal marker. Two diluents were made and each in turn injected twice into an inert column which had previously been heated to a known temperature . The delay in exit from the column at the other end was measured by a detector system and each chemical had its own retention time on the column. The retention times for alcohol and propanol are different and the area under the peak generated by the detector is related to the quantity detected.

A variant of the technique was "head-space chromatography" in which the vapour above the sample of fluid is analysed, .and this overcame the problem of the clotted sample but other problems remained.

There remained the problem of samples which had been;–

1. Subjected to heat in an attempt to force the sample to "clot" and so make it unsuitable for analysis. It was easy to detect this because the heat caused the colour of the blood to change from red to chocolate brown.

2. Tampering with the sample. Sometimes it seemed that normal blood had been injected into the tube so as to dilute the alcohol in the sample This was suspected when the concentration of alcohol that we found was in fact considerably less than that found by the police. We could usually confirm the suspicion by observing scuff marks on the container which showed tampering. we could follow up our suspicions by comparing the concentrations of other chemicals (urea, creatinine,

sodium, potassium) in the blood sample given

to us with what was in the police sample.

R. The role of the expert witness

It is essential that the expert witness understands that he has a duty to the court to be impartial;. although called by one side in the first instance he is not acting for either the defence or the prosecution but is in Court to explain the technicalities of his report.

Initially the expert is approached either by the driver of the vehicle or, as is more usual, his solicitor. I need to have all the relevant information, including the height and weight of The driver and all the information about the breath or blood test that was carried out by the police, and the circumstances that led up to his arrest. I would then write a report to the solicitor (or driver) giving my opinion concerning whether he has a valid excuse. If the solicitor wants to use my report in Court, he sends it to the prosecutor who may in turn send it to his own chosen expert for possible comments and any rebuttal., Eventually he decides wether to accept my report in toto and   want me to attend the trial for cross-examination. Alternatively my report might not help the defence and may not be used at all. My experience has been that provided my points are taken, attendance at court is often not required. However, if the the point being made is contentious, as was frequently the case in those   cited below, another expert might be called by the prosecution. For example this was certainly so in the trial of the man with thrush of the tongue, described later.

At first I was asked only occasionally to go to court and give my expert opinion on these questions, but as time went by the number of enquiries that I received gradually increased, and I became recognised as a true expert. Since about 1980 I had been receiving 2 or 3 enquiries a week from solicitors requiring my expert opinion on some facet of drink-driving cases, and must have issued hundreds of reports and attended hundreds of court trials. Consequently I must have heard just about all the reasons that motorists have used as excuses and in addition I have proposed some new ones, some of which are described below.

However, I should first briefly explain that in about 1997 we sold the laboratory to another company, but Peter Liu bought the alcohol section snd retained me as consultant. Later when Peter got too busy because of the London Gender Clinic he sold on the alcohol section to Ron Kasidas, and he too retained me as consultant.

The remainder of this book describes examples of the ways in which drivers have attempted to avoid losing their driving licences, plus some amusing instances. In reading them one should appreciate that they constitute a minute fraction of drink-driving offences. Most offenders find it best to plead guilty and accept the consequences. However, a small proportion elect to go to trial and of those, a small number obtain "not guilty " verdicts or are granted special reasons for not losing their driving licences.

S. "I know this expert witness"

The expert witness has an obligation to be impartial, and likewise the Judge or Magistrate has an obligation to be unbiased in assessing the evidence given by the expert witness. On two occasions I have found myself in the position of being known personally to the Judge or Magistrate.

Case 1. This was in the days when drink-driving charges could be held before a judge in the Crown Court. On being called to the witness box to give my evidence, after giving my qualifications the following conversation took place;—

Judge: Does that mean you are an Oxford man?

Me: Yes your honour.

Judge: Were you by any chance at Wadham College?

Me: Yes your Honour.

Judge, turning to the prosecutor: I have to confess that I know this witness; do you have any objections to thetrial continuing?

Prosecutor: Your honour, I am a Queen's College man; we have had problems with Wadham before but I think I do not have to object on this occasion!.

It was then that I realised that behind the Judge's wig, there was a face that I knew from our college days.

Case 2. In the morning of the trial I realised that the presiding magistrate was the Father-in-law of my daughter. As I would not be giving my expert evidence until after lunch, I decided to make myself known during the recess for lunch. However, the Magistrate had spotted me sitting in the Court, and declared that he knew me, just before breaking for lunch. Again, the prosecution were informed and raised no objection.

T The laced drinks defence.

The law allows that the Magistrates may find the driver guilty but allow special reasons why he should not lose his driving .licence. The onus is on the driver to prove his case. Someone must be prepared to come to Court and attest that he did indeed lace the drinks, be quite clear on exactly how it was done and with what, and how much of it was added. It s then for the expert witness to calculate what the breath alcohol level would have been had the lacing not happened. Several cases come to mind. However, these cases should put into perspective. The vast majority of drink-drive offences are conceded with the driver pleading guilty. Of those that plead special reasons, about a half are refused special reasons, but below are some of those who managed to keep their driving licences.

1. A journalist thought he had finished work for the day and walked to his local to meet friends and enjoy a drink. One friend thought he was a bit down that night, and having been told he had finished work laced his drinks with vodka. A bit later he was

called on his mobile telephone by his newspaper to attend a certain scene. Our journalist, not knowing that his drinks had been laced went home, got out his car and rushed to the scene. His friend had not been about when the telephone rang and did not realise that he would be driving that night. Result, our Journalist was stopped for speeding and found to be over the legal limit for Driving.

2.. Mr CT drank a single glass of wine with some snacks at a party at 10 to 11.30 PM. Before driving again he checked his breath alcohol on a personal instrument and found it to be 10 ug per 100 Ml. He drove to a pizza restaurant where he drank half of a 330 ml bottle of 5.2% alcohol beer. He then drove to his flat where he found in the refrigerator a meal of chicken in a tomato and chili sauce made by his Finnish cook. Using a Finnish recipe, she had added exactly 400 ml of vodka into the sauce after the chicken had been cooked. She ate one portion herself and left the other equal portion for her client. CT ate his portion cold and quite quickly afterwards he drove off in his Ferrari only to be stopped by the police at 12.35 AM. An evidential breath test at 1.40 AM showed 52 ug of alcohol per 100 ml

As I knew exactly how much spirits he had unknowingly consumed I was looking forward to explaining to the court that he would have been below the legal limit but for the spirits in the sauce.

It was not to be. On the morning of the trial, the defence team were all present but no police officers arrived. It was at a time of tension due to various bomb attacks and the police failed to inform the court that they could not attend. The magistrate was very cross and demanded that the police officers attend on him to explain their failure. Moreover he dismissed the charges and ordered £1000 costs against the police. Mr. CT took the defence team across the road to a pub and ordered a bottle of champagne to celebrate.

I sent my fee note to the solicitor and awaited payment. It did not come even after a reminder. I therefore wrote to Mr. CT telling him that I had taken him to be an honourable man but nevertheless I had not been paid. By return of post my cheque arrived with an apology, explaining that he had not been told about the outstanding bill. The cheque was signed by a Lord of the realm!

.

3. An amusing case which ending with it being dismissed.

Mr. D had drunk 2 pints of beer and was correct in his belief that this would not have put him above the legal limit for driving. He then stopped off at his Father's house which was quite nearby. His father had made a chocolate cake and into the mix had added A quantity of a liqueur which he had carefully measured out. The cake was consumed completely, the Father eating one quarter and Mr. D consumed three quarters. Mr.D left to drive elsewhere completely unaware that the cake had contained alcohol. He was apprehended by the police, given a breath test and was amazed to find that the alcohol level was slightly over the legal limit, and

I calculated that the 2 pints of beer would not have put him over the limit, but the additional alcohol in the cake neatly explained the figures that the police obtained. This meant that he could plead special reason for not losing his driving licence, but in fact the magistrate took an even more lenient view and dismissed the case.

Case 4

In this, as in most cases, the lacer usually chooses vodka for the lacing because, when mixed with other drinks, taste is not affected and neither is it detectable on the breath.

Mr. V attended a family celebration at a restaurant. Knowing it was going to be a long night he decided to take his overnight bag and stay the night, and had informed everyone o f his decision. A friend decided that he needed a bit of cheering up and laced his drinks with vodka. However Mr. V decided in the

e

course of the evening that he would not stay the night and left to drive home. He of course did not know that his drinks had been laced, and his friend did not know that he had decided to drive. Mr. V. was stopped by the police and found to have breath alcohol well over the legal limit and was charged.   Later, he learned that his drinks had been laced and went to Court where he successfully pleaded special reasons for not losing his driving

U. The "hip-flask" defence.

This describes the situation in which after the accident the driver is given brandy or other spirits, or the driver walks home and takes or is given spirits. Then I might be asked to calculate what his alcohol level would have been had the post-driving alcohol intake not occurred. This is often rejected by the court for lack of proof that he did actually drink after the accident. However, occasionally the proof is there as in the case below.

Mrs. X had taken lunch with a friend during which she had drunk 2 glasses of wine over a period of about 2 hours. She then drove towards her home, but on the way collided with another car as a result of which her car was not drivable and was towed away to a garage. Mrs. X then went home where she met three friends who plied her with wine. An hour or so later the police arrived at her home and required a sample of breath which was over the legal limit for driving. A subsequent evidential breath test confirmed that the alcohol level was indeed over the limit.

In court. three of her friends gave evidence that at home she had been given by them at least three glasses of wine. I calculated that without this wine she would have been well below the legal limit. This was accepted by the Magistrate and consequently she was found to be not guilty.

V. "Failure to provide" a sample as required

This is the charge made if a driver is unable or unwilling to provide a specimen of breath for alcohol analysis. The penalty is the same as if the breath alcohol had been found to be over the the legal limit

A successful plea was made by Mrs FK. She had drunk a single glass of wine before driving to meet her husband. On the way home she suffered a head-on collision with another vehicle as a result of which she was knocked unconscious, had a bleed-iing nose, head injuries. and sustained considerable bruising of her chest from the seat belt she had been wearing. Photographs were produced in court that that clearly showed the extensive bruising of the chest. Regaining consciousness quite quickly she was taken to the police station for an evidential breath test. The Police Surgeon agreed that a breath test should not be attempted because of pain on deep breathing and recommended a blood test. However blood could not be obtained because all of her veins were collapsed, and I maintained that this demonstrated that she was still in considerable state of shock at the time. Urine was then requested but she was unable to produce any. It was thought she was unwilling to provide a urine sample, but I stated in Court that if she was indeed in shock and her peripheral veins had collapsed it was likely that kidney function was also temporarily impaired and that there might not have been any urine in the bladder to pass. She was found not guilty..

W. Asthma is frequently given as a reason for not being able pro

vide a breath specimen. The intoxilyzer currently in use by the

police is the "6000". It requires a minimum of 1.2 litres of breath

which should be delivered at a steady flow rate of at least

12 litres per minute (200 ml per second). Therefore the first thing

to investigate is the lung functions of the driver. These test are

usually carried out at the lung function test department of the

local hospital, asking in particular for ;–

Forced expiratory volume in 1 second (FEV_1) which is

probably the best indicator of ability to satisfy the requirements

of the breath testing equipment. Nevertheless it will still remain

to be shown whether or not the asthma was in a similar medical

state on both the day of the hospital test and the day of the

police test

In my experience,most trials based on this defence fail be

cause had the driver been in an obvious asthma attack at the

police station, they would have been asked to provide blood or

urine.

X. The "rape" drug, Rohypnol

In the following two cases I went to Court expecting the defence to be hopeless, but events revealed the almost certainty of rape drugs having been an important factor.

Case 1.   Mr. B was in the company of one friend and two others whom he did not know. Between 6 and 7 PM he drank 4 pints of Carling draft lager They then went elsewhere and he drank 2 pints of lager and a single brandy and coke.   He   remembers nothing more until a policeman knocked on the door of his car, and he remembers only bits of what followed later.   A subsequent evidential breath test showed 52 ug of alcohol per 100 ml. The police reported that his car was well out in the countryside and pointing away from his home.

Shortly afterwards he attended his own GP because he could not understand what had happened. A sample of urine had been analysed at the local County Hospital and been found to contain both Morphine and Zopiclone (a sleeping drug), but these had never been prescribed for him and he had never knowingly taken them. Rohypnol was not found, but of course would have disappeared from the body by then.

His bank contacted him and reported that in the night of the incident an attempt had been made to withdraw money with his cash card, but since the wrong PIN was given none was obtained... Moreover he had no recollection of his cash card having been stolen and it was in his pocket the morning after the incident.

The explanation put forward was that his drinks had been doped to enable the malefactors to rob him of his cash card, but having been unable to use it had replaced it in his pocket and let him go, whereupon he drove without knowing where he was going. He was acquitted in the Magistrate's Court of the charges against him.

Case 2. Miss K. During the evening she drank bottles of fruit juice and water. Between 11.30 PM and midnight she drank a bottle of Smirrnoff ice (black). At about 2.50 AM while driving was stopped by a Police patrol and a subsequent blood test showed 88 mg alcohol per 100 ml. The defence was to be that her drinks had been spiked by a person unknowns and she had indeed left her drink unattended while she went to the toilet. She remembered nothing from that time until she woke up in a police cell.

However, in Court the sergeant who had arrested her confessed to being rather uneasy. He had spent considerable time acting as under cover agent in trying to stop malefactors using the rape drug on unsuspecting young ladies. He thought he recognised the signs of this drug on Miss K, but failed to follow up the matter with a blood test for the rape drug because the Police station was so busy on that night and he did not remember to do so until it was too late. She too was acquit ted with a warning to watch her glass and not to leave one unguarded when in a public place.

Y. The changing problem of the hiatus hernia.

The abdominal cavity is separated from the chest by the diaphragm. However in order to reach the stomach ingested food has to pass through this diaphragm and this is accomplished by a one-way valve system. Unfortunately it is quite common for this to fail in such a way that food can regurgitate up the oesophagus and even reach the mouth. This is sometimes referred to as a hiatus hernia.. The patient knows about it because the acid con tents of the stomach cause a burning sensation when food reaches the oesophagus (commonly called heartburn) and an acid taste in the mouth when it reaches the tongue..

This impacts on drink-driving cases because if the driver has reflux of stomach contents into the mouth and then blows into the breathalyser, alcohol from the stomach may result in an artificially raised readout of alcohol in the breath. In fact I Believe that I was the first person to raise this as a defence against in a drink-drive trial.

Case of Mr. MG.. At a restaurant with a friend he drank two 175 ml glasses of Merlot wine. He asked for the bill and went to the toilet. On returning to his table he saw a cup of coffee with cream on the top. Not having ordered this he was told it was complimentary. Later he found out that it contained 35 ml of whisky. While driving home he was apprehended by the police who thought (wrongly as it happened) that his car had bumped the wing mirror of a parked vehicle. An evidential breath alcohol showed 54 ug alcohol per 100 ml (legal limit 35). He had suffered from hiatus hernia with gastrro-oesophageal reflux for many years and the diagnosis had been proven by gastroscopy and biopsy. During reflux he experienced a burning sensation in his throat and mouth. He had been suffering from the reflux immediately before the breath test. He therefore pleaded guilty, but with special reasons for not losing his licence. The conditions required seemed to be satisfied;–

1. The whisky was drunk at 12.30 AM and the breath test

was at 1.20 AM , so that he would have had alcohol in his stomach at the time of the test.

2. He had the burning sensation in his throat and mouth immediately before the breath test.

3. The breathalyser in question was tested and found not to record mouth alcohol when alcohol was actually in the mouth.

In the Magistrate' Court, as often happens when the matter is too technical for them to understand, he was found guilty, but later in the Crown Court he was granted special reasons for not losing his licence.

However, as time passed the reflux defence underwent scrutiny and certain conditions were deemed necessary in order to be accepted as the cause of the blood or breath alcohol being over the legal limit in drink-drive cases.

1. There had to be alcohol in the stomach at the time of the breath test. This would only be so if stomach emptying was not complete, and this might take say 1½ hours without a previous meal, to say 3 hours after a heavy meal.

2. There had to be clear evidence that reflux actually occurred. A clear medical history might suffice but evidence from a gastroscopy with or without biopsy would greatly help.

3. There had to be clear evidence that reflux into the throat or mouth had occurred just prior to blowing into the breathalyser.

The Lion Intoximeter 3000 was not good at recognising

mouth alcohol, but a few years ago it was replaced by the 6000 machine which was supposed to recognise mouth alcohol when present. This should have ended the problem but failed to do so and it has been shown that most of these machines fail to recognise mouth alcohol. even when deliberately put into the mouth. Consequently there continued to be many cases in which the defence was "mouth- alcohol for pleading special reasons for keeping their driving licences

Change in the law.

It was decided in a case heard at the High Court that any thing that was breathed into the breathalyser came from the lungs and was therefore suitable for analysis. This completely ignored the fact that it could have been mouth alcohol that was being measured. Therefore the finding of mouth alcohol over the legal limit did not prevent a driver from being found guilty. This flies in the face of common sense, but nevertheless remains the basis of the law until it is changed by a higher court, presumably the House of Lords. In the Author's opinion this a clear case of ""the law is an ass". Nevertheless, mouth alcohol can be the basis for pleading Special reasons for keeping their driving licences.

Z. Abnormal metabolism of alcohol

Case of Mr. DW. On the night before his alleged speeding offence he drank 5 or 6 pints of beer between 8 PM and mid night. The next day, 7th June, he drank two 400 ml cans of cider at 12.30 PM. He was stopped for speeding and a subsequent evidential blood alcohol level at 7.48 PM showed 94 mg alcohol peer 100 ml..

Being a biochemist he thought it odd that he was over the legal limit for driving and went to see his GP asking for liver function tests. In fact the tests on 12th July showed markedly raised liver enzymes which implied impaired liver function. Since alcohol is metabolised almost exclusively in the liver he thought that this might explain his delayed fall in blood alcohol level. To find out if this was so, on 3rd September, between 1.35 PM and 2.22 PM I gave him 250 ml of vodka (equivalent to 10 single pub measures) well diluted with water and the results are as shown

Table 1. Effect of giving DW sufficient vodka (275 ml of 37.5% alcohol, vv, equivalent to 10 pub measures) between 1.35 and 2.22 PM on blood alcohol levels at various times

Time of day (PM)	Blood alcohol mg per 100 ml
1.35	Zero
3.17	71.4
3.47	92.5
4.22	120
4.52	134
5.25	135
6.14	113

These   results   are   remarkable   in   two   ways;–

A. Absorption of alcohol was not complete until over 4

hours after he began drinking the alcohol, a

time much longer than expected.

B. Between 5.25 and 6.14 he suddenly developed an

Abnormally fast rate of fall of blood alcohol of 29

mg per 100 ml per hour (Normal 10.4 to 24.2

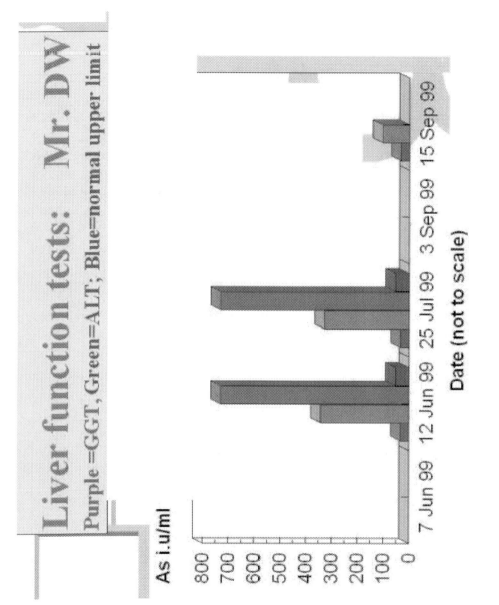

On 15 th September another blood test for liver function showed normal results. In conclusion, it did seem that he had abnormally delayed metabolism of alcohol as late as September and his alcohol metabolism would presumably have been even more abnormal back in July when his liver function tests were far more abnormal.

.

.

1. The case of the secret drinker.

Mr. I.H. was unfortunate enough to cause a police car to brake sharply to avoid a collision at a round-about. The police alleged further erratic driving and therefore stopped an spoke to him. Having observed a strong odour of alcoholic liquor, a roadside test showed over the limit and a subsequent evidential breath test showed 125 ug alcohol per 100 ml of breath (about 4 times the   legal limit). It was curious that with so high a level of alcohol, he showed very few sign of intoxication.. He was referred to me for observation of his behaviour at the level of breath alcohol found by the police.

He assured me on arrival for the test that he had taken no alcohol for three days., but nevertheless his blood alcohol on arrival proved to be abut 100 mg per 100 ml. I calculated that to raise his blood alcohol level to 286 mg per 100 ml (equivalent to the breath level found by the police) would require 515 ml of 0% vodka, which is equivalent to over 10 pub doubles.

I

However after he had drunk 200 ml of the vodka his blood alcohol had risen to 250 mg per 100 ml and I decided to give him no more vodka. On examination at that stage he showed almost no signs of alcoholic intoxication other than slight difficulty successively placing of one foot in front of the other.

Clearly he was used to high levels of breath alcohol, and this was supported by the finding of a higher than usual rate of fall in blood alcohol level after the peak had been reached. He insisted that he had taken no alcohol for the 3 days prior to the test and I therefore considered the possibility that he might have the Autotbrewery syndrome in which yeast in the intestinal tract generates alcohol (see below). It was agreed that on another day he should attend for a glucose loading test to see if this would cause a rise in blood alcohol. He duly arrived with his father who assured me that they had spent the night under the same roof and he, the father was quite certain that his son had no access to any alcohol. The son insisted that he had abstained from alcohol for 6 days but nevertheless his fasting urine alcohol proved to be 88 mg per 100 ml (equivalent to 66 in blood). I gave him a dose of 75 grams of glucose in the form of "lucozade". This was followed by a steady decline in the urinary alcohol level and no rise whatsoever. It was then my painful duty to report to the father that his son was a secret drinker and had better plead guilty to the charge of drink-driving

2. The role of the alcohol loading test

Sometimes there appears to be a great discrepancy between the measured level of blood or breath alcohol on the one hand, and on the other hand the state of intoxication record ed at the time by the police and/or other observers. In this case I might be asked by the defending solicitor to give the driver enough alcohol to reach the level found and observe his state of intoxication.

At other times there may be doubt about his actual rate of fall of blood alcohol after raising the blood level to the observed value. The rate of fall is linear (constant) during the period after absorption is complete. The average rate of fall of blood alcohol in the post-absorptive state is 17.2 mg per 100 ml per hour, with a range of 10.4 to 24.2 ug per100 ml per hour..In breath,the average rate of fall in the post-absorptive state is 7.5 ug per 100 ml per hour, with range of 4.5 to 10.6 ug per 100 ml per hour.

The carrying out of these loading tests requires the simultaneous presence of myself to administer the calculated amount of alcohol to be given and also to take the blood samples, Dr. Kasidas to analyse the blood samples, and of course the driver charged with the drink-driving offence. I have to observe the analyses of the samples by gas chromatography so that I can give evidence upon the results in court, so sparing Dr. Kasidas' time.

In order to calculate the rate of fall of the blood alcohol level we need to find three consecutive points on the graph in a straight line and then measure the slope of the line.

In the course of carrying out a hundred or more of these loading tests we have seen many different types of effect induced by alcohol. In general they conformed to the guide lines published by the British Medical Association in the early days of the drink-driving laws which are quite useful and quite easy to Remember. At a blood level of;−

100 mg per 100 ml, **di**zzy and **d**elightful

200 mg per 100 ml, **d**runk and **d**isorderly

300 mg per 100 ml, **d**ead **d**runk.

400 mg per 100 ml, **d**anger of **d**eath.

However, people do vary and there were some striking exceptions to these guide lines some of which are described below.

Two drivers with very high blood alcohol levels showed almost no signs of intoxication. The first was a market gardener who was arrested near his farm in the countryside at about mid night when he drove a very short distance. The police who had arrested him reported that he appeared quite sober and in fact he had to show the police how to get back to the police station as they had got lost. Imagine their surprise when the breath test showed an alcohol level of well over the equivalent of 400 mg per 100 ml ("danger of death").

I was therefore asked to raise his blood alcohol level to the level found and assess his behaviour. In fact we were as surprised as the police had been to find that at that blood alcohol level I could scarcely find any signs of alcoholic intoxication. I subsequently attended his trial and was able to state that although he had had such a high alcohol level, in my opinion he probably was not a threat to the public when driving. He was spared the prison sentence he could have received, but was banned from driving for 2 years.

The second habituated driver was a steeple-Jack who found that he needed a strong drink to give him the courage to do his job. Gradually the dose require had mounted as he be came adapted to high blood alcohol levels. Eventually he was apprehended by the police while driving and the evidential blood test showed an alcohol level of well over 400 mg per 100 ml.. Since no-one had considered him to be drunk at the police station I was asked to carry out an alcohol loading test. The result was quite clear; at the high blood level of well over 400 mg per 100 ml, he showed virtually no signs of Intoxication.

At other times we saw the reverse effect. For example, a respectable bank manager had been found to be quite sober despite a very high blood alcohol level. We were never able to load him up to that level of blood alcohol because he mentally disintegrated before our eyes well before we got to the desired alcohol level. H e was completely disabled by intoxication, unable to walk unaided and clearly utterly drunk. I had to get him by taxi to a railway terminus in London, install him in a seat and explain to the Guard the problem and ask if he would kindly put him off the train at his destination.. He arrived home safely but remembered nothing of the journey.

One driver who was fairly reserved before the alcohol loading changed remarkably as his alcohol level rose. First, he became complimentary Then became loquacious in praise of what we were doing, and then as his blood alcohol rose became insulting and eventually fell asleep. Later he offered his deep apologies for his behaviour.

I was sometimes asked in Court if the defendant had been acting drunk. I am confident that this was not so for three Reasons'

. First I never tell the driver in advance what result I am looking for, and I also ask the solicitor to observe the same rule when he tells the client what is proposed.

Second because some of the tests for sobriety are not at all subjective and not under the driver's control.

Third, but by no means least, as will be gleaned from the above, I have a large and perhaps unrivalled experience of seeing how drivers do react to rising levels of alcohol.

114

3. Rare medical conditions which affect the charge of drink-driving.

   i. Autobrewery syndrome. This is a rare condition, first described in Japan, but it has also been seen in Europe, and in the UK in particular. There is often a history of long term treatment with oral antibiotic therapy. These antibiotics can sterilise the normal intestinal flora so resulting in overgrowth of yeast which then begins the fermentation reaction which converts glucose to alcohol and carbon dioxide,

   Mr. FS is the only case in which I have been able to prove the existence of this condition. I had always hoped to find a second case which would have made it attractive for publication in the scientific press. However, I have not yet found a second case so I am publishing details of the first case here.

   FS was adamant that he had consumed no alcohol for at least 24 hours before his arrest on 11th September. He had drunk moderately on 10th September but had finished drinking   by midnight. On 11 th September he collected his girl friend and saw a film at a cinema. Afterwards they went for a drive. After parking his car he was questioned by a policeman who wanted to know why he had driven in a bus lane. Following failure of a roadside breath test he was given an evidential breath test which showed 66 ug alcohol per 100 ml of breath (legal limit 35).

He remained adamant that he had not been drinking and moreover, his girl friend who seemed a most honest and law-abiding citizen, backed up his story completely.

The defence seemed to have no case, but I was struck by his medical history. He had suffered from digestive problems for many years, and had been investigated by Doctors in Belgium from where he originated. They had suspected liver disease and had given him multiple and prolonged courses of antibiotics. All of this was confirmed by correspondence with his Belgian doctors. It seemed to me that as a result of the antibiotics he might also have disturbed metabolism of alcohol if he in fact had liver disease. I therefore proposed to carry out both an alcohol loading test as described above, and also a glucose loading test to establish whether or not he converted the glucose to alcohol.

I carried out the two tests on the same day with the glucose loading test first. He had taken no alcohol for 3 days and on the day of the test he took a light breakfast of croissant and milk at 7.30.. A preliminary blood test at 10.07 AM showed zero alcohol level. I then administered 75 grams of glucose given as Lucozade, 450 ml between 1024 and soon after 10.40 AM. I took further blood samples at 11.23 AM and 12.24 PM. Both showed zero alcohol and at that point I wrongly concluded that he did not have Autobrewery syndrome, and I then started the alcohol loading test in which I gave him 294 ml of Whiskey (40% v/v) between 12.35 and 1.58 PM. The resulting blood tests are shown in table the table overleaf.

Time of day	Blood alcohol as mg per 100 ml
2.47 PM	158
3.16 PM	157
4.46 PM	185
5.46 PM	184

I had calculated that the alcohol administered should have given him a maximum peak blood alcohol level of 160 mg per 100 mat about 2.30 PM. This level did occur at the expected time of about 2.30 to 2.45 PM, but to our great surprise, in stead of falling thereafter as expected. the blood alcohol kept on rising and even at 5.46 PM it still exceeded our target level, thereby showing that more alcohol was in his body than we had put in.. This seemed to prove that he was generating alcohol in his body, presumably due to fermentation of the glucose having got under way after a time delay of several hours. I explained to him the importance of the observation and that it would be helpful if he would allow me to search his body and clothing for occult alcohol. He readily agreed but I could find no evidence that he had secreted some alcohol somewhere and drunk it with out our knowledge.

It would have been of great interest to have continued the observations for longer, but by 6 PM he had had 8 blood samples and I doubted that he would tolerate more and so we had to stop the study at that point. Likewise a blood sample the next morning would have been useful, but then we would be unable to prove that he had taken no alcohol overnight.

In court, we put forward the defence that the alcohol in his body was not due to drinking it as required by the act of Parliament and that therefore he could claim to be not guilty of a drink-driving offence. The magistrate was not happy about accepting this, but I explained that we had excluded all other possibilities and the only explanation for his raised blood alcohol was Autobrewery syndrome. This was accepted by the court and the driver was found not guilty.

119

As far as I know this is the only time that the Autobrewery syndrome has been successfully used by the defence in a drink-driving trial.

However, looking at the results in the case of FS, it is apparent that had we not continued to observe his blood alcohol levels for some hours after the glucose loading test had been concluded, we would have missed the diagnosis. It seems clear that we should have considered the possibility that it might take some hours for the fermentation reaction to get going. In retrospect it seems likely that we may have missed other cases in the past through not waiting sufficiently long.

ii. Thrush of the tongue. A defence too far!

RS attended a police station for reasons which have nothing to do with the case. There it was noticed that he had an odour of intoxicating liquor on his breath, a roadside breath test showed over the legal limit and an evidential breath test showed 57 ug per 100 ml (legal limit 35).

It transpired that on the day of the alleged offence he was suffering from a serious thrush infection of the tongue and two days later he attended on his own Doctor who made the diagnosis and cured it with an appropriate antibiotic.

I proposed the defence that thrush, being an infection with yeast could have generated alcohol and given rise to a localised autobrewery syndrome, and that therefore as in a true autobrewery syndrome he could have been not guilty of having had excess alcohol present *due to having drunk the alcohol.*

The prosecution called their own expert who rebutted my Proposal on the grounds that the amount of yeast present on the tongue would have been insufficient to have generated the level of alcohol In the breath on two successive blows into the machine. The problems I had were;–

1. Thrush on the tongue has never before been shown to generate alcohol, although it seems self-evident that it would, or could.

2. Thrush of the tongue had been cured by his doctor before I had an opportunity to test the idea by measuring his breath alcohol level with and without the presence of thrush.

3. I could find no evidence in the medical literature to show that thrush on the tongue actually had given rise to alcohol generation

I pointed out to the court that just because a condition has never been described it does not mean that it doses not exist and that in view of the ease with which thrush is cured it is not surprising that it has never been tested for alcohol production.

Therefore, my defence was rejected both at the Magistrates Court and a subsequent appeal. However, I still maintain that thrush of the tongue could have been the cause of the alcohol observed, but it not going to be easy to prove the point.

3. Megacolon, a rare cause of stomach reflux.

The term "Megacolon" is used here to describe a number of rare congenital conditions leading to failure of the large bowel (colon) to function properly, causing it's enlargement. The result is a build up of waste material in the colon which can back up into the small bowel and thence to the stomach. When the full-blown picture is present it can endanger life, but mild conditions occur as in the case described here.

GH arrived at a pub at about 7.30 PM. He ate a meal accompanied by a "lager top" and a 175 ml glass of wine. He then set out for home by car but was stopped by a police patrol car At 9.45 PM. An evidential breath test at 10.48 PM showed 77 ug alcohol per 100 ml (legal limit 35).

I first calculated that his expected breath alcohol at the time he was tested should have been about 14 ug per 100 ml. He then gave a history of reflux of stomach contents into the mouth and I therefore decided to take a medical history from him and this proved most remarkable.

For as long as he could remember he had had digestive problems. Unaided by medication a meal caused his stomach to "blow out" causing regurgitation of food into his mouth for hours during which he tastes the food over and over again, and also suffered from bad breath. In addition he had extreme difficulty with his bowel movements. This is such a feature of his life that prior to the alleged driving offence has had never complained about these problems to his own doctor. Since then however he has consulted his doctor who prescribed laxatives with a dramatic relief of his symptoms.

I made a tentative diagnosis of Megacolon and proposed that with great delay in stomach emptying, the alcohol he drank at the restaurant had remained in his stomach until the breath test and that the regurgitation into the mouth resulted in an incorrect breath alcohol reading as described in detail above.

At the magistrate's court it emerged that he was well known at the pub where he had dined for his curious eating habits. Witnesses described how he might have a large meal and then not eat for days. He was found guilty at the magistrate's court, but at appeal to the Crown Court he was granted special reasons for not losing his licence.

iv. inhalation of alcohol; can it account for being over the legal limit?

In general, the answer is no because the vapour pressure of alcohol in blood is greater than the vapour pressure of room air. However circumstances were unusual in the case of PL. He had been working from 5.45 AM to 10.30 AM in a very small closed attic room with no ventilation. He was trying to find a new method of making self sealing rubber balloons and he had been coating them with alcohol by using a rag that had been saturated with alcohol in a bowl immediately in front of him At 11.15 AM he was stopped by a police patrol for speeding and a subsequent evidential blood test at 12.50 PM. showed 91 mg per 100 ml.

Since the vapour pressure of alcohol at 25c is 59 mm of mercury,the maximum concentration of alcohol in room air would be 132 mg alcohol per litre of air. However, the maximum concentration that the human can accept without irritation of the airways is 20 mg per litre (Lester etc al, Quart. J. Studies Alc

1951, <u>12</u>, 167. Since he suffered no untoward irritation I esti-
mated that he was breathing in up to 15 mg of alcohol per
litre for some 4.75 hours. I then calculated that this intake
could have raised his blood alcohol level by about 36 mg per
100 ml. Therefore, had he not inhaled this alcohol the blood
alcohol found by the police would have been 91- 36= 55 mg
per 100 ml which is well below legal limit for driving. This
argument was accepted in the Magistrate's Court and he was
granted special reasons for not losing his driving licence.

AC. Closing thoughts on some of the above cases

The reader may get the impression that some of the drivers who escaped the charge of drink- driving, and that this can be an easy option. However, I would strongly advise them that it is no easy option.

First a driver needs a strong defence based on facts which must stand up to scrutiny by other experts.

Second, the trial may be delayed for many months, and even after that an appeal may take more months before it is heard. Overall, final verdicts may not be known for over a year, during which the defendant suffers greatly from not knowing what his fate will be. Many find this very trying.

Third, most defendants are found guilty. This may have knock-on effects. A driver may lose his livelihood if it is dependant on driving. When he eventually gets his licence back he will almost certainly find that his insurance premium has gone up very considerably, and take years to get back to the previous raring.

The moral cannot be stated too often or too loudly,

Do not drink
and drive

Index

Printed in the United States
By Bookmasters